Dick Johnson
7/13-91

Cover Design: Carole Westhuis
Calligraphy: Carole Westhuis

*The beauty of Carole's calligraphy
is appreciated by everyone who enjoys the poetry.
Without her, we would be less than we are.*

Address inquiries to:
Rhymes For Reasons
P.O. Box 5010, Suite 175
Asheville, N.C. 28813

Table of Contents

This is my second book of poetry.

The first, copyrighted in 1987,
was titled "From the Heart" and included
my first eleven poems.
All of that poetry is included in this book as well.

There is one more thing that I've repeated this time . . .
the dedication.

These are the people who make it all worthwhile for me.
These are the people who are my life.
There's no one I would rather pay tribute to
with my work.

Dedicated . . .

To my Wife - my inspiration...my motivation...
my love. You make me want many tomorrows.

To my Children and the special people with
whom they share their lives. God knows how
much I love you all...I tell Him about it
everyday. I hope you know it too.

To my Grandchildren - You fill me with such
pride. I know God loves me, there can be no
doubt, because He gave me you.

To loyal Friends - You stood at my side when
that was not a very fashionable place to be.
I pray that I can be as good a friend to you.

I Write

I write because of wrongs I've done
    For which I must atone.
I write for others who've made mistakes
    Lest they too feel alone.

I write about winning and losing
    And the price we pay, either way.
I write about thinking - and choosing
    The path to a brighter day.

I write about caring and sharing
    And keeping love alive . . .
About trying and sometimes failing,
    But continuing to strive.

I don't have all the answers,
    But what I feel, I share.
I write because I hope to help.
    I write ... because I care.

The thing that started all of this was a poem titled, "The Things I Want for You". It represented the very first time I even thought about writing poetry. It was born out of the worst thing that ever happened to me in my life – out of the most crushing defeat I've ever had to face - out of the pride I felt in having survived all of that, and out of the great truth that I learned from that experience. It was written for our 5 wonderful children and for their children - out of my love for them – and with the prayer that my words would help them learn from my experience.

The Things I Want for You

I want you to hurt, so you can learn to cry...
I want you to fight, so you can learn to try.

I want you to lose, as I know you must, with a smile
  still on your face.
I want you to win and never gloat, but win with
  style and grace.

I want you to know who and what you are, and what
  you want to be.
I pray when you look in the mirror each day, you'll like
  the one you see.

There's so much that I want for you, so much that
  you must learn...
Like love ... love's not a thing you get, but something
  that you earn.

And pride...pride doesn't always come from winning...
  standing tall ...
There's pride that's found in what you do in failure,
  when you fall.

You see, to fall, to make mistakes...in that there's
  no great sin.
The loser is the one who falls... and won't
  get up again.

In retrospect, I am amazed at how much my sense of values has changed over the years.

There was a time when success, fame and fortune... things... were the best I felt I could hope for in life.

Now, although I continue to strive for success, I know that, whatever happens, I already have the most valuable thing I could ever hope for... the sure and certain knowledge that... I am loved.

I am Loved

If my life has peace and quiet calm,
　　It's all because you're here.
All that I know of beauty and love
　　I've learned since you've been near.

If I know that I have value,
　　It's because you made me believe.
I can set aside all of yesterday's wrongs,
　　I need no longer grieve.

If all my tomorrows hold promise
　　That yesterday wasn't there,
It's because I don't have to face them alone,
　　You'll be here with me ... to share.

If all my doubts and fears are gone,
　　There's a reason, all others above,
It's because I'm complete – I am fulfilled
　　I'm whole now ... I am loved.

Several years ago, my son-in-law presented me with a very special gift. It was a copy of "Footprints in the Sand", done in calligraphy. I love it so much and have always wished that I had written those beautiful words.

More significant than the gift itself, was the statement his giving it made with regard to his attitude toward me and our relationship. He had seen me, very successful in broadcasting, much too macho and full of myself to ever take much stock in anything as gentle as simple faith in God. He had seen me fall from the level of success I'd achieved and end up with little more than my family to hang on to. He'd seen me accept the losses I'd brought on myself, never blaming others for my failure, and he'd seen me rise up and rebuild the life that I had almost destroyed. He never turned his back on me and, in giving me this gift, he was telling me that he respected what I'd come to believe in and that he respected me. That is a special gift. The poem, "My Friend God", was inspired by that gift.

My Friend God

A very large part of what I am
  And what I can hope to be
Can be found in the fact that You are here
  And in lessons that You've taught me.

You taught me to listen
  You taught me to care.
You taught me to laugh and to love
  And to share.

You taught me I'm never defeated
  'Til I give up and no longer try.
You taught me to know that one man's joy
  Is another man's reason to cry.

You taught me that no one's perfect –
  That no one always wins.
That everyone falls short sometimes
  And everybody sins.

You taught me that You are always here
  That You care when I feel pain.
You taught me that there, within every loss,
  Lie the seeds of a much greater gain.

I remember the day I first reached out to You
  And I felt my torment end.
I will always be grateful, always give thanks
  To You . . . my God . . . my Friend.

There are those tortured souls, I am one of them, who are doomed to spend their lives counting calories. If you're with me on this, you know what a curse it is.

Through no fault of my own, I've managed to keep things under reasonable control over the years. The credit - or blame- depending on how you look at it, must go to my wife. She is relentless in her determination to keep me around as long as possible. I guess she cares about this old pelican.

I know that left to my own devices, any diet I undertook would go about as follows.

The Diet

This is the moment it all begins
   A brand new slender me.
I'll take off thirty pounds and be
   The best that I can be.

I won't surrender. I'll never give up
   Until I'm down to size.
I can just see people looking at me
   With envy in their eyes.

To think that I could do all that.
   Throw off that heavy yoke.
I'll celebrate by ordering . . .
   Chocolate cake - and diet Coke.

As a grandfather, I find that I've been given the opportunity to look at life from three different perspectives – through three sets of eyes, so to speak.

I watch my grandchildren... growing... learning... always impatient to get to each new level in school... to the drivers' license... to the things that, to them, mean freedom. They seem to be in such a hurry to grow up.

I watch my children... so busy with careers... homes... friends... the kids. There never seems to be enough time to fit it all in - but-somehow they do.

As for myself... I can remember being where they are, with all the hopes and dreams ... enduring all the struggles. But now, I find myself wondering... where did all that time go? How did it pass so quickly? Wasn't it only yesterday that I started my life's journey.

Time

When we are young
    We see time as our foe,
It passes too slowly it seems.

The impatience of youth
    Makes us wish time away
As we yearn to start living our dreams.

Then time changes its pace
    There's just never enough
In the years we spend learning and earning.

There's so much we must do,
    So much to get through
But those hands keep relentlessly turning.

When we are old
    We see time as our foe,
It passes too swiftly it seems.

There's so little left
    And yet . . . just yesterday
We set out in search of our dreams.

I was, for many years, a radio and television sports announcer. During that time I had the pleasure of being close to the "Glory Years" Green Bay Packers and to the man who led them, the legendary Vince Lombardi. Those were great times. Traveling with the team to the first two Super Bowl games and getting to know those great athletes and their outstanding coach was an experience I will never forget.

Most memorable to me was Lombardi. He was, in my opinion, the greatest football coach who ever lived. He was, to me, a study in contradictions. He could be spectacularly profane, but was a very devout man, a daily communicant. He drove his players with an intensity that bordered on cruelty - but - he was, as far as I could tell, always completely fair in the way he treated them. He was a man who loved to laugh - but - could fly into rages that were frightening in their intensity. He was a man who would have succeeded greatly in any field he might have chosen... And who literally forced the men who played for him to reach deep within themselves to find the greatness that he knew was there.

My poem, "The Winners", deals with a piece of Lombardi philosophy I have always remembered and have always wanted to write about.

The Winners

We all look up to the Winners,
Those who stand above the rest.
We long to be numbered among them—
To prove to the world we're the best.

We struggle and strive - we give it our all-
Pay the price - do whatever it takes.
When we come up short, we get up and go on,
Having learned from our mistakes.

And then ...when we get to be Winners,
When that circle we finally join...
We learn a lesson all Winners must learn-
There are two sides to every coin.

We learn when we win - when we're at the top,
The prize is ours just for today.
With each new dawn, there'll be someone along,
Who'll be trying to take it away.

When we win and prove that we're the best,
That isn't the end, because then,
We've got to go back tomorrow...
And prove it all over again.

I remember, as if it were only yesterday, standing in a darkened room where the only illumination came from a small night light. I was looking down into a crib where our first born child, then only 2 weeks old, slept peacefully.

So much went through my mind as I looked down at that little face... so many questions:

Would I be all that I should be for her?

Would I be able to give her a good life?

Would I be able to make her proud of me?

Could I, somehow, find the wisdom to do it right?

That tiny baby is a grown woman now with three children of her own. We've never talked about it, but I'm sure that she and her husband, like young parents throughout

time, have stood, looked down at those helpless little people, and said their own parents'
prayer.

A Parent's Prayer

I gaze at that beautiful, innocent face
   untouched by life's problems and pain...
Like new canvas awaiting the brush of time,
   fresh and clean as a warm spring rain.

I feel love, I feel pride ... some fear is there, too.
   as I think about all that could be ...
As I think of the pitfalls that life can bring...
   as I think of the things you must see.

I pray that I'll always give you enough,
   but never give you too much.
I pray I can teach you to have enough faith
   so you'll never lose hope or lose touch.

I pray I can set an example
   that will teach you to love and be true.
I pray I'll remember, when you fall short,
   that I was young once, too.

I pray that I'll have the patience
   to listen when you speak.
I know if I don't, I can never hope
   to give you the answers you seek.

All of my prayers will be answered,
   on the day that you go your own way,
If you'll just stop a moment - look in my eyes -
   and say... "Thank you, you showed me the way."

I have a friend I've known most of my life. I also have a brother. They are the same person.

I realize that isn't unusual, but I think the way we arrived at our relationship is. You see, we really never knew one another as brothers. We had the same father -but- we never even lived under the same roof. We never saw each other more often than every three or four years.

A few years ago, circumstances brought us together for an entire year. During that time we spent every minute we could together. We worked together, played together, laughed together and often sat up till dawn just talking. We, at last, became brothers in the true sense of the word.

My poem, "A Friend Is", was written with my brother and his wife very much in mind. I feel truly fortunate to be able to say that they are the best friends we have.

There are few things more valuable in life than a good friend. This poem reminds me of mine. I hope it will make you think of yours.

A Friend is ...

A Friend is a gentle presence
   Bringing comfort when things go wrong.
A Friend says words that lift me up
   When I need help to be strong.

A Friend is there to help me
   Bear my pain when I am sad.
A Friend enjoys it with me
   When I win ... when I am glad.

A Friend holds out encouragement
   When I struggle and I strive.
When all seems lost, my Friend is there
   To help keep hope alive.

That's what Friends are for, I guess—
   They're there to see us through.
And there's nothing that you've done for me
   I wouldn't do for you.

I know, my Friend, we share a Prayer
   That God above will bring
To my Friend ... a life of peace
   And happy songs to sing.

One of life's hardest learned lessons can be found, clearly stated, in those undying words... "There ain't no free lunch".

That wise, albeit ungrammatical piece of wisdom prompted me to write the poem I call "Deserve".

If you feel you deserve
   much more than you've got,
Then consider what
   many have learned ...
We rarely receive
   what we think we deserve,
We get only the things
   we have earned.

You'd think that a poem for an adopted child would be very difficult for someone with no personal experience in that area...but... it was easy for me.

I had the pleasure, over the years, of seeing three adopted children come into the lives of my wife's sister and her husband. I saw the joy those kids brought to them.

Remembering all that love and happiness was all the inspiration I needed to write this poem.

The Chosen One

A whole new dimension and meaning
    Was added to our love.
The day you came into our life –
    A gift from God above.

You brought our lives fulfillment,
    Brought new purpose to our days.
Through you we see life's beauty
    In all new and wondrous ways.

There may be greater gifts I suppose,
    But I can think of none.
You're the answer to our every prayer,
    Our child . . . our chosen one.

If we're lucky, life will bring us someone to love. I have been lucky.

I wrote the untitled poem I call "Caring" one night after my wife had gone to bed. It was on the eve of our 34th wedding anniversary.

My fortunes were at low ebb at that point and I really couldn't afford to offer her much of a gift the next day. So, I sat at the kitchen table and put the love I felt into the words you are about to read.

My fondest wish for you is that you read these words and realize that you feel this way about someone, too.

Often, when I'm all alone
        and can daydream for awhile,
I think of the love that God gave me
        I remember ... and I smile.

I think of the day I met you,
        how I liked you from the start.
How your smiling eyes and easy laugh
        reached out and touched my heart.

I remember all the times we laughed
        and also the times we cried.
But happy or sad ... good or bad
        we faced them — side by side.

That's what it's all about, you know
        the loving ... the touching ... the caring,
The joy and sadness ... laughter and tears
        the winning and losing ... the sharing.

I don't know what tomorrow may bring;
        we're not allowed to see,
But I know I can face it unafraid
        because you'll be there with me.

I talked to my son on the phone last night and came away from that conversation feeling very good. It wasn't so much what he said that gave me that feeling... It was the way he said it.

I knew, just from the sound of his voice, that our boy had arrived at a place we've always wanted our children to be. The poem I've titled "Respect" should explain what I mean.

Respect

When I was defeated and wracked with pain,
  I was weak because I cried.
When I celebrated the things I'd done,
  That was the sin of pride.

When I had given my best, but lost,
  I hadn't done all I could.
When I had fought my battle and won,
  I was lucky, and not that good.

I wanted, so much, to please everyone
  Till I learned that never can be.
I know now the first step to being complete
  Is to like... and feel good... about me.

Now, when I win and I feel that pride,
  That feeling is something I've earned.
Now, in defeat, I don't hang my head,
  I tried... it's a lesson learned.

Now, when I look in a mirror
  And gaze at the face it reflects...
I feel no concern for what others may say.
  If that's somebody I respect.

I've seen many sad things in my life, but none sadder than the treatment accorded the men and women who served in Vietnam when they came home.

It was shameful !

I do not mean this to be a statement of support for our involvement over there... but...

I definitely do mean this to be a statement of support for a group of brave Americans who stood up for what they believed in and did what they thought was right.

I think those who castigated them and spat upon them when they came home should be ashamed of themselves.

I think we should all be ashamed that those things were allowed to happen.

I know the lot of the Vietnam Vets has

improved… but… not enough has been done.

In that regard, all I can say is – it's about damned time.

My Heroes

I stand at the wall, my eyes fill with tears
    As I read that long, sad list.
So many... so young... so much promise -
    They're gone now, it's come to this.

I think of those who served and survived,
    Then came home to find hearts hard as stone.
It seemed no one cared about all their scars -
    They weren't welcomed... they stood alone.

Their country had called and they'd answered
    What she asked was what they did.
Now, they found themselves less respected
    Than those who just ran and hid.

How can there be shame in doing your best ?
    They fought and they suffered and died.
Right or wrong, they stood up for what they believed,
    They went to Vietnam and tried.

I don't give a damn what others may think,
    They are, and they always will be...
Numbered among our bravest and best...
    Among those who are heroes to me.

If you have traveled any distance at all along life's road, you've probably faced a situation sometime where you needed help in one way or another. Living presents us with so many pitfalls, temptations and opportunities to make mistakes, it's no wonder that nearly everyone has been in that position.

It's different for each of us and we can see it in as many different ways.

For me it was people who stuck with me when I was down... who believed in me when I went completely wrong... and who loved me when that had to be a very difficult thing to do.

But most of all, it was a God who reached out to someone completely unworthy and gave me a reason, and the strength, to go on trying. How can we ever repay someone who's done that for us ? You can, in your own way, and I can with the words I write, try to Pass It On.

Pass It On

You, my true and steadfast friend,
 Never turned your back on me.
You saw value in this tortured soul
 That no one else could see.

You helped me step out of my shadows,
 To stop clinging to what might have been.
You made me see what tomorrow could be,
 And you showed me how to begin.

You stood by my side when I struggled
 In my quest for a brighter day.
You watched me fight and learn and grow
 Till, at last, I have found my way.

With all of my pain behind me now,
 With my doubt and my fear all gone...
I'll thank you by doing just what you'd ask...
 I'll try to pass it on .

"Take My Hand" was written, in its original form, to be included in the church bulletin at our daughter's wedding. I wanted, in honoring this beginning marriage, to make a statement with regard to my feelings about the commitment that was being made, and about what the future inevitably holds for young couples starting out together. It isn't always easy – but, with love and with luck and a whole lot of honest effort – wonderful things can result.

I feel I can speak with some authority here – because it happened this way for me.

Take My Hand

Take my hand — come walk with me
   Along life's winding way.
Take my hand — come stand with me
   Together we will say:

It's you that I have chosen;
   It's you with whom I'll stay.
It's you with whom I'll share my life,
   I want no other way.

I want you always by my side
   Through laughter and through tears.
The good — the bad — we'll share it all
   Through all the coming years.

Because I want this union
   To continue to be blessed,
I pray we both will care enough
   To always give our best.

I know that if we do our best,
   Then when our journey ends,
We'll find that we've come through it all
   Still lovers... ever friends.

My childhood was an unconventional one. I was brought up by my father's sisters, two unmarried school teachers. Later in life my dad and I came to understand and love one another. But, all those early years, those two wonderful ladies were the ones who took on the task of being parents to a sometimes hard-to-handle young boy.

I honestly never felt shortchanged, never gave much thought to having missed anything because of those circumstances - but then- I married.

Entering my wife's family circle was a revelation to me. Her gentle and devout father helped me to learn about the power of faith and love -and- that it's okay for a man to cry. Her wise and understanding mother helped me to realize that it's possible to disagree while still respecting another's point of view and that a bit of gentle humor is often the best way to calm troubled waters.

Just spending time with my wife, her three younger sisters and her mom and dad, added a whole new meaning to the word "family" for me.

When I wrote the untitled poem I call "Parent", I had all of the people I've mentioned here in mind:

> My Dad - I love him and still miss him and I know he did the best he could. My wife's mom and dad, who so generously took me into their family.

> And most of all, my beloved Aunt Esther and Aunt Ruth who gave me all the love any little boy ever needed.

Today, in a quiet moment,
In my mind's eye I saw your face.
I thought of the ways you've touched my life
And made it a better place.

When I was small, confused and scared,
You offered a safe place to hide.
When I was bad, you still loved me –
When I was good, you took pride.

When I was young and headstrong
And had to have my way,
Your strength and gentle wisdom
Stopped my going too far astray.

When I was wrong, you taught me
To stand and pay the price.
You taught me the wisest can make mistakes –
But it's fools who make them twice.

There are so many ways, I can't count them all,
That you helped me and guided me through.
The word Parent means discipline, caring and love.
The word Parent … to me … means you.

My assignment that cold March night in Milwaukee was to meet the Marquette University basketball team returning from a road game, their last regular game of the year. I was to obtain an interview with their coach, Al McGuire, who was about to lead them into another appearance in the NCAA tournament.

I missed them. Missing an interview for a radio show may be painful - but - it's never been fatal to anyone I know of. But, in spite of that, I was about as discouraged as a man could be as I walked shivering in the cold, back to my car.

My reaction was heightened by the fact that I was going through a terrible time in my life. I was trying to climb out of a very deep hole I had dug for myself and this failure just added to my already unbearable load. I was thinking that it was all hopeless. . . that I might as well give up and quit trying.

At that moment a big black car with dark tinted windows pulled up to the curb beside me. A man got out, walked over to me and said, "There's a guy in the car who wants to talk to you." Apprehensively, I walked over to the car... opened the back door and there sat Coach McGuire. He gave me my interview then and there.

Al has probably, long since, forgotten that ever happened. I never will.

That tough guy from New York knew of my struggles and pain. He held out his hand that night, doing what he could to help. He made my struggle just a little easier, and in so doing, taught me something that I now pass along to you with this poem.

Thanks Al.

Tomorrow

As another day comes to an end
   And I lie down for my rest,
There's a question I must ask myself,
   Did I do my very best ?

Did I touch some lives along the way,
   Try to make them better and brighter ?
Did I help make someone's path smoother ?
   Did I try to make someone's load lighter ?

Did I remember lessons learned
   In days that had gone before ?
Did I give each task my very best ?
   Could I have done much more ?

I know, though I tried, that I did things wrong
   And while there's regret, there's no sorrow.
Those mistakes are the reason I want to go on
   To all I'll do right ... tomorrow.

When we're very young we tend to look at life through rose-colored glasses, convinced that we have the answers and, supremely confident of our indestructible future.

I wrote "The Secret" remembering what it was like to feel that way, and from the realistic perspective of one who, like everyone, every where, has hit a few bumps in the road along the way.

If we've lived, we've learned that bad times come to us all - and - if we're lucky we've also learned that most of our growth comes, not from triumph, but from tribulation.

The Secret

I stand here now looking back at my life
And it comes as no surprise –
Things haven't been anywhere near as smooth
As I saw them through innocent eyes.

I thought life's road would be level and wide
I thought it would never bend.
I thought that when good things came my way
The good things would never end.

Then I learned it doesn't work that way –
Good fortune can't always be mine
I learned that I can't always win –
That my Sun won't always shine.

I learned that when I come up short,
I should waste no time with sorrow...
But, get myself back on my feet
And try again tomorrow.

Discouraging? Maybe, but think about this –
It's a Secret I've come to know...
I've learned very little while sitting on top –
But Adversity made me grow.

Do you remember Toto, the little dog from the movie, "The Wizard of Oz"?

For 15 years I had a dog that was a dead ringer for Toto; she could have been a twin.

Time took its toll on my little friend and one day, I couldn't fight it any longer; I had to take her and have her put to sleep.

I must tell you, that was one of the hardest things I've ever done.

Out of that painful experience, I wrote, "I Miss Her".

I Miss Her

A good friend of mine
      Has gone away.
She won't be back...
            And I miss her.

There are those who'll say
      She was only a dog.
I suppose they're right...
            But I miss her.

She was old and sick,
      Tired and gray,
Much too tired to play...
            Gee, I miss her.

Letting her go
      Was so hard to do,
I guess I knew...
            How I'd miss her.

While there's comfort in knowing
      Her pain is gone,
Mine goes on and on...
            'Cause I miss her.

Back in those days when I earned my living as a television sports announcer, I mentally composed a brief poem dedicated to newspaper critics everywhere. It just never made sense to me that people who had never done what I was doing had any right to judge my work.

In the beginning it angered me... Later I stopped caring, concluding that the audience would dictate my future, regardless of what the critics had to say. Today, I realize that every person in every job has at one time or another, felt exactly the same. Since we are all in the same boat, I decided to include that piece of work in this collection.

I'm growing very weary
Of being shown the light
By people who can't do what I do,
But know I'm not doing it right!

If there's a theme that runs through my work, I suppose it would be the idea of getting up again when you fall… learning from mistakes…growing through adversity.

I guess that's because this is a subject I know about. I have been there.

I fell … just about as hard and as far as a person can fall. Now, one of my greatest sources of pride is the fact that, despite it all, I never quit.

I've spoken on the subject in hundreds of schools, at conventions, before gatherings of all sorts… always trying to help people realize that they can win, no matter how hopeless things may look.

I've seen it happen to others… I've lived it.

There isn't much that I believe in more completely than the inestimable value of trying … one more time.

One More Time

When it seems like the whole world's against you,
    When you're nearing the end of your rope,
You might feel like throwing in the towel
    'Cause you can't see a reason to hope.

Don't let yourself think about giving up,
    Don't walk with your head hanging low.
Remember, it's learning from your mistakes
    That helps you gain wisdom and grow.

You're only human, you'll suffer defeats,
    We all must bear various crosses.
Don't judge yourself by the fact that you lost,
    But the way that you handled your losses.

When your path seems too hard and you just can't go on,
    When to try there's no reason or rhyme . . .
Remember, the sweetest success of all
    Comes to those who try. . . .one more time.

I have always been a little envious of people who, from childhood, were completely at ease in their spiritual lives. That was not true in my case.

I don't know why.

Maybe I thought I wasn't worthy. Maybe I thought I was so strong that I just didn't need it.

Whatever the reason, I fought it until I was almost 50 years old.

Thinking about all that, I knew I wanted to write something to tell that story.

If you are struggling as I did… I wrote this poem for you.

Finding God

I remember thinking I needed no God,
  Not believing there was one there.
But that kind of thinking just brought me a life
  That was burdened with pain and with care.

I remember looking at those who'd found God,
  They all seemed so joyful - so free.
I thought, am I wrong ? Is there really a God ?
  If there is, would He do that for me ?

I remember calling out to God
  Through my pain and despair and defeat ...
And He heard me ... He touched me and lifted me up,
  Helped me make my life complete.

Now, everywhere I look I find God ...
  In the forests and in the skies ...
In helping hands, in caring hearts,
  In smiling, loving eyes.

God's here ... He's there ... He's everywhere
  And He wants to help us through.
If you're hurting and struggling, call out to God ...
  He's just waiting to hear from you.

It seems to me that most parents are pretty much the same in at least one way. We all want the very best for our children.

Many of the problems that occur stem from our getting so caught up in giving them "things" that we lose sight of what would be of far greater value to them.

We cannot buy self respect, the respect of others, or happiness for our children - but - we can give them the capacity to achieve these things.

We cannot, for any price, guarantee our children lives free of failure, pain and defeat - but - we can give them the freedom to make mistakes and learn from them - to face defeat and bounce back from it - and to suffer pain and learn to cope with it.

We can, if we do it right, help our children to become complete human beings. I can think of no greater legacy.

The Legacy

There are gifts you can give to your children
 That have value far greater than gold.
Gifts of faith and hope and strength and love
 They'll forever cherish and hold.

The gift of a home full of laughter and love
 Where they'll learn the fulfillment of sharing.
Compassion for others enduring great pain,
 So they'll learn of the joy found in caring.

The courage to stand up for what they believe,
 Even though they, at times, stand alone.
The strength to admit to wrongs they have done,
 And the willingness to atone.

The wisdom to know when it's time to speak,
 And to know when to listen and learn.
The pride to be taken in work done well,
 And in the respect they have earned.

These precious gifts are yours to give.
 Give them ... and you'll always be
Proud of your children and what they've become,
 Because of your legacy.

All of us have, or will someday, suffer the pain that comes with losing someone we love. These are among life's most difficult moments.

Several people who touched and helped to shape my life are gone now. I miss them.

I wrote the poem you are about to read in their memory. It is the best way I can think of, remembering what I had with them, to say goodbye.

Some light has gone out of my life.
     I see darkness
     I feel sorrow.

You've gone away.
     Without you here
     How can I face tomorrow?

I know I can't.
     I know I must
     I know you'd want me to.

I know . . .
     Remembering all we shared
     Will help me make it through.

So I'll bear my pain,
     And somehow
     Find my way through all my sorrow.

I'll smile when remembering
     You once were here . . .
     And I'll reach out for tomorrow.

- Goodbye -

I remember my Grandma.

I remember a gentle lady who spoke with a heavy Swedish accent.

I remember how she could make the hurt go away with a warm hug, a quiet word, or one of her loving smiles.

Most of all, I remember that care-worn face. To me it will always be one of the most beautiful I've ever seen.

It was remembering that very special lady that moved me to write " Faces".

Faces

I've traveled far along life's road . . .
    I've seen many things and places.
My fascination never ends
    With the things I see in faces.

The faces of the very young,
    So open . . . free of guile
With eyes that say I trust . . . accept,
    Always ready with a smile.

The faces of the wounded . . .
    They reveal how much they grieve.
Their eyes reflect their desperate need
    For a reason to believe.

The faces of survivors . . .
    Those who've made it through their storm.
They've fought their fight . . . they've paid their price
    And now they're safe and warm.

The beautiful faces that I love the most
    Are the faces of the old.
Those lines . . . those dimming eyes
    Reveal the memories they hold.

I see character and wisdom
    Gained through years of joy and strife.
They help me see what I might be
    When I too have lived a life.

I'm often asked how long it takes me to write a piece of poetry. It varies. Some go quickly... some take weeks in development.

There is one that I wrote in exactly five minutes. It's the poem I call "Blame".

The idea came to me while watching the Contra hearings on TV. It occurred to me, as I listened to those people, that they probably wouldn't find anyone to blame for that situation... no one in any position of serious authority. Unfortunately, I was right.

I felt sad as I wrote these words, sad to think that this is what we are becoming.

These days, if you fail -
It won't matter.
Everything stays just the same.

All you must do
Is keep smilin' through -
And find somebody else
To blame.

I have been through some bad times in my life, and I've learned that much of the pain we experience is self inflicted and that, in most cases, it didn't have to happen at all. All too often, we do it to ourselves. I've learned that, whether we realize it or not, we all have choices to make everyday, choices that can dictate the quality of life that we live... the quality of the life we can build for the people we love.

I've learned that while God and family and friends can, each in their own way, help us to survive our mistakes and failures and pain... they cannot do what must be done for us... we must do it !

"My Life Is" is about choices and trying and about where the responsibility for our lives must ultimately be placed.

My Life is...

Walking alone and
feeling lost in dark
and stormy weather

or

Facing that storm holding
someone's hand, knowing
we're in it together.

It's feeling small
and helpless

or

Standing tall and proud.

It's whispering in
a timid voice

or

Speaking clear and loud.

It's failing and falling
and making mistakes
and giving up and crying

or

It's failing and falling
but getting back up and
going right on trying.

It's following down a
shadowy path, one who
seems certain and strong

or

It's going the way I
know is right, though
others tell me I'm wrong.

It's seeing the burdens
that others must bear,
never helping set them free

or

It's helping and caring
and loving and sharing,
being all that I can be.

As I stand here now, gazing down two paths,
I know I must choose one and take it...

There's one great truth that I can't escape-
My life will be what I make it.

You may recall my earlier reference to the role my Dad's two older sisters took in bringing me up. Those two beautiful ladies will be a treasured memory for me until the day I die.

They were both teachers, and I can remember how hard they tried to help their students find joy and excitement in learning. They were dedicated to, and loved very much, the work they did. They truly cared about those kids.

That memory undoubtedly contributes greatly to a warm spot I've always had in my heart for teachers. I don't think I've ever talked to any successful person who couldn't recall a teacher or teachers, who had struck a spark in them in some way and started them on the road to achievement.

That, I submit to you, is what good teachers do.

A Teacher

A teacher just asks for the power
    To reach out and touch young minds...
For the wisdom to show the way to go
    And what's better left behind.

A teacher in looking at children,
    Doesn't see them as gifted or slow.
A teacher sees young people, just starting out,
    Who must learn in order to grow.

A teacher will criticize gently,
    Lest a child give up on believing,
Always aware that a thoughtless word
    Could end striving and achieving.

A teacher knows we are all different,
    That your dream may not be for me,
So we're taught to think and always search
    For the place that we should be.

A teacher instills a desire to learn
    And pride in work well done.
A teacher knows that seeds planted today
    Bloom tomorrow as races are run.

So often, when speaking with people who've read my work, I hear the comment, "Those are my thoughts, exactly. I wish I could put them into words."

Needless to say, it's gratifying to be told something like that... and it occurred to me that I should write something for these folks.

This is the way I think they might say it.

Speaking of Love

There's so much I want to say to you,
    Things I feel deep in my heart.
Those feelings overwhelm me,
    But I don't know where to start.

I would write a poem to show my love
    But I don't know how to say it ...
Or a beautiful song for only you,
    But I don't know how to play it.

So there'll be no poem – no beautiful song
    To speak of the love that I feel.
All that I have to offer is me,
    And a love that is boundless and real.

My poem will be patience and gentleness...
    My song, love that's faithful and true.
May all that I am and the best I can be,
    Be the least that I ever give you.

Four of our five children are girls. Brought up in the same home, by the same set of parents, they should be very much alike, right ?

Forget it !

Each is her own person...

Each has chosen her own path...

They are very different, with one very important exception. They have a common concern for each other and for their brother.

They keep in touch with each other.

They're right there when needed.

They are the people who made me realize how very special a sister can be.

The Gift of a Sister

Even though there were times we disagreed,
    She's the one who was always there
To rejoice in my good fortune,
    My pain and sorrows share.

She knows me for what I really am,
    All that's good and all that's bad,
But right or wrong, she stands by me,
    The truest friend I've had.

Where she is, I always feel welcome.
    Where she is, I have a friend.
Where she is, there's sanctuary,
    Where acceptance and love never end.

I've been granted so many blessings,
    And one of the greatest must be
A gift that has added so much to my life...
    A sister was given to me.

What do you think is the very best thing you can hope for in life ?

That's called a dream.

It's beautiful when those dreams are realized... but... don't bet the ranch on it.

I'm not saying that you shouldn't dream, but that you should be realistic in your expectations. I believe that you should accept who you are and what you have without giving up on being better and having more. The chances will come...You must sieze the moment.

We start out thinking
   "The world will be mine."
Then life teaches lessons . . .
   That dream's left behind.
We discover life's not always fair.

We live with laughter.
   We live with tears.
We're joyful and hopeful.
   We're filled with fears.
If we're lucky, somebody will care.

We walk in darkness.
   We walk in light.
Our days can be cloudy,
   Or sunny and bright.
Good and bad . . . that's what living must be.

We keep asking why
   It can't always be good,
Why it can't always be
   What we thought it would.
The answer is there, clear to see.

We Are Given Our Moments

Conventional wisdom states that the only things that any of us can be completely sure of are death and taxes. I would add one more thing to that list of inevitabilities... change.

Looking back, I'm amazed at the number of changes I've gone through... I'm even more amazed at their scope. If ten years ago, you'd have asked me to list a thousand things I might be doing today, writing a book of poetry wouldn't have even made the list.

Life is change -

Think about it.

Moving On

As it must to all
The time has come
For a phase of your life to end.
You've traveled so far
On this part of life's road
But that road is about to bend.

Now you must turn
And walk away
But that's just the end
Of an inning.
Today marks the end
Of one phase of your life...
~ Tomorrow ~
A whole new beginning.